KU-544-662

Play with ART

For the grown-ups:

This book is full of hands-on arty ideas to help children explore their creativity as they experiment with different materials. For each creative media section, there is a handy "tools needed" catalogue and 6+ projects to try. Just lay out one set of materials at a time, then your child is ready to go – and parents only need to clean up once!

Safety

Children should be supervised at all times when doing these projects. They may need help with some of the trickier activities such as cutting cardboard. Always ensure your child uses non-toxic paints and materials.

Mess alert!

Some of the projects will make a mess (that's part of the fun)! Protect the area where your child is creating – or even encourage them to do the projects outside. Wearing old clothes or an apron is advisable.

Mess alert!

We made this book:

Violet Peto

Rachael Parfitt Hunt

Rachael Hare

Lol Johnson

DK | Penguin Random House

Editor Violet Peto
Senior Designer and Illustrator Rachael Parfitt Hunt
Designer and Illustrator Rachael Hare
Photographer Lol Johnson
Additional Photography Dave King
Design Assistance Eleanor Bates, Charlotte Milner
Jacket Designer Rachael Parfitt Hunt
Jacket Co-ordinator Francesca Young
Producer, Pre-production Rebecca Fallowfield
Producer John Casey
Managing Editor Penny Smith
Managing Art Editor Mabel Chan
Publisher Mary Ling
Art Director Jane Bull

First published in Great Britain in 2018 by
Dorling Kindersley Limited
80 Strand, London WC2R 0RL
Copyright © 2018 Dorling Kindersley Limited
A Penguin Random House Company
10 9 8 7 6 5 4 3 2 1
001–305904–March/2018

All rights reserved.
No part of this publication may be reproduced, stored in or introduced into a retrieval system, or transmitted, in any form, or by any means (electronic, mechanical, photocopying, recording, or otherwise), without the prior written permission of the copyright owner.

A CIP catalogue record for this book
is available from the British Library.
ISBN: 978-0-2413-0182-1

Printed in China

A big thank you to all the models – Edie Arnold, Oscar Arnold, Archer Brandon, Betty Johnson, and Lola Johnson

A WORLD OF IDEAS:
SEE ALL THERE IS TO KNOW

www.dk.com

C903194336

Play with ART

templates

Trace or copy these **templates**
onto thick paper and cut them out.

Contents

8 Painting and printing

10 Mix the colours up!

12 Printing gallery

14 Fruit and veg fun

16 Block buddies

18 Fingerprinting gallery

20 Handy hands!

22 Funny feet!

24 Pop! Art

26 Masking out

28 Paper crafts

29 Paper folding

30 Paper cutting

31 Paper sculpture

32 Paper caterpillars

34 Fan-tastic

36 Shadow puppets

38 Stained glass elephant

40 Wet paper art

42 Drawing and colouring

44 Animal doodles

46 Chalk art

48 Scratch art magic!

50 Make and create

51 Colour matching game

52 A tower of tubes

54 Rainbow mobile

56 Magical unicorn

58 Shadow theatre

60 Cardboard collage

Painting and printing

Experiment with **paint** to create different **effects.**
Here's what you need:

Paper

Roller

Roller tray

What shall we paint?

Canvas (or thick paper)

Funnel

Masking tape

Printing inks

Clear zip-up plastic bag

Glue

Non-toxic paint

Felt-tip pen

Pencils

Paintbrushes

Cardboard tubes

Balloons

Balloon pump

Your FEET!

Bubble wrap

Wooden blocks

String

Sponge

Flowers

Top tip
Your hands and feet are great printing tools!

Fruit and veg

Peg

Pom-pom

Paper plates

Your HANDS!

Your FINGERS!

Washable plastic toys

What colours shall we choose?

9

Mix the colours up!

Do you know how to make **new colours**?

Primary colours

 RED YELLOW  BLUE

You can **make** new colours by mixing the three main **primary** colours.

Try these mixtures:

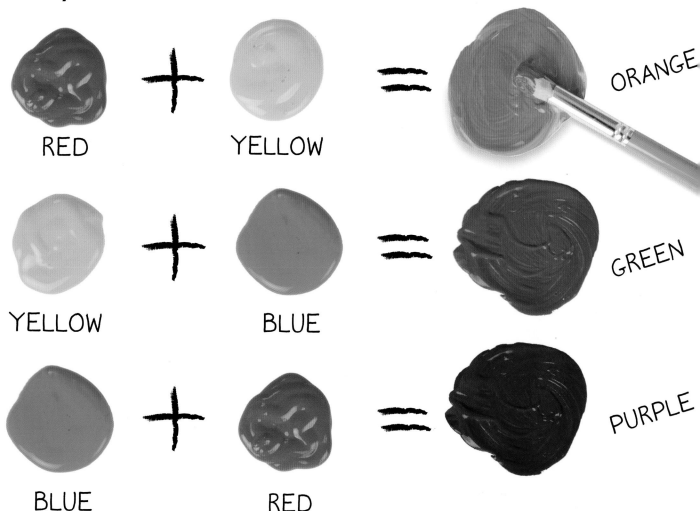

RED + YELLOW = ORANGE

YELLOW + BLUE = GREEN

BLUE + RED = PURPLE

10

Make your own colour wheel

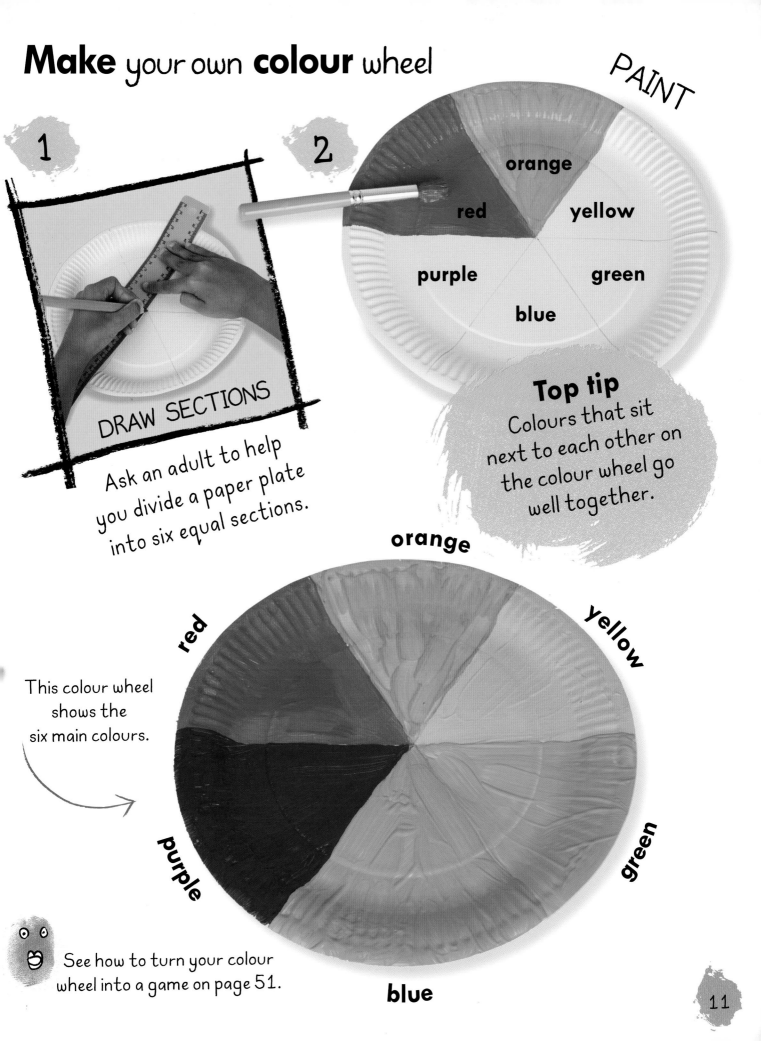

1

DRAW SECTIONS

Ask an adult to help you divide a paper plate into six equal sections.

2

orange

red

yellow

purple

green

blue

Top tip
Colours that sit next to each other on the colour wheel go well together.

This colour wheel shows the six main colours.

orange

red

yellow

purple

green

blue

See how to turn your colour wheel into a game on page 51.

11

Printing gallery

Create lots of paint **marks** using different printing **tools**.
Here are some ideas:

Bubble wrap feet

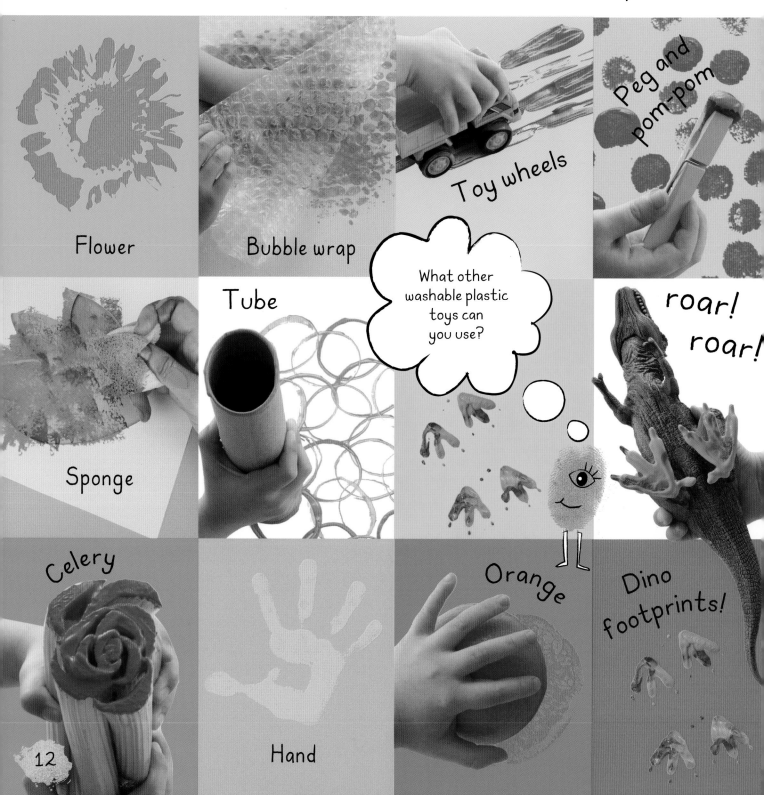

Flower

Bubble wrap

Toy wheels

Peg and pom-pom

Tube

What other washable plastic toys can you use?

roar! roar!

Sponge

Celery

Hand

Orange

Dino footprints!

12

Make your own **printing** blocks!

Tools needed:

Wooden blocks

Foam or thick card shapes

You can find heart and star templates at the back of the book.

String

Glue and paintbrush

Roller and paints

1

GLUE

Glue your foam shapes onto wooden blocks.

2

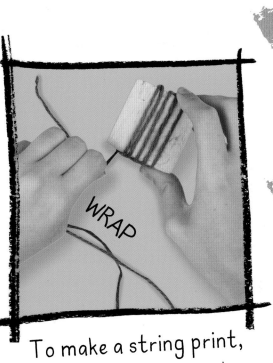

WRAP

To make a string print, wrap string around a wooden block.

3

ROLL

Using a roller, roll paint over your printing blocks.

4

PRESS

PRINT

Print different patterns and shapes to make wrapping paper or cards.

13

Fruit and veg fun

Use **fruit** and **veg** to make amazing **art.**

Tools needed:

Non-toxic paint

Paper

Pencil

Fruits and vegetables

Paintbrush

1

PAINT

Cut the fruit or veg in half and paint the flat side.

Top tip
Print a cool poster to hang on the wall.

2

FUN shapes

PRESS

Start printing! Make lots of lovely, colourful patterns.

Use a pencil to give me eyes and a mouth.

PRETTY patterns

Block buddies

Make colourful people by painting with **wooden blocks** and **potatoes.**

Tools needed:

Paper and coloured pencils

Halved potato

Wooden blocks

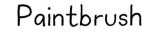

Paintbrush

Use other sides of the block for different colours.

1

PRESS

Paint the side of a block. Press down onto paper for the bodies.

Why not use blocks to give me arms and legs, too?

2

PUSH

DOWN

Use a halved potato to make the head shapes. When dry, draw on funny faces.

Top tip
Use different sized potatoes for big and small heads.

Fingerprinting gallery

You can use your **fingers** and **ink** to make many marvellous pictures.

Use a pen to give us funny faces.

Tools needed:

Paper

Fingers

Felt-tip pen

Mess alert!

Printing inks

Press your finger on the ink pad, and then onto paper. Use a pen to make the prints come to life.

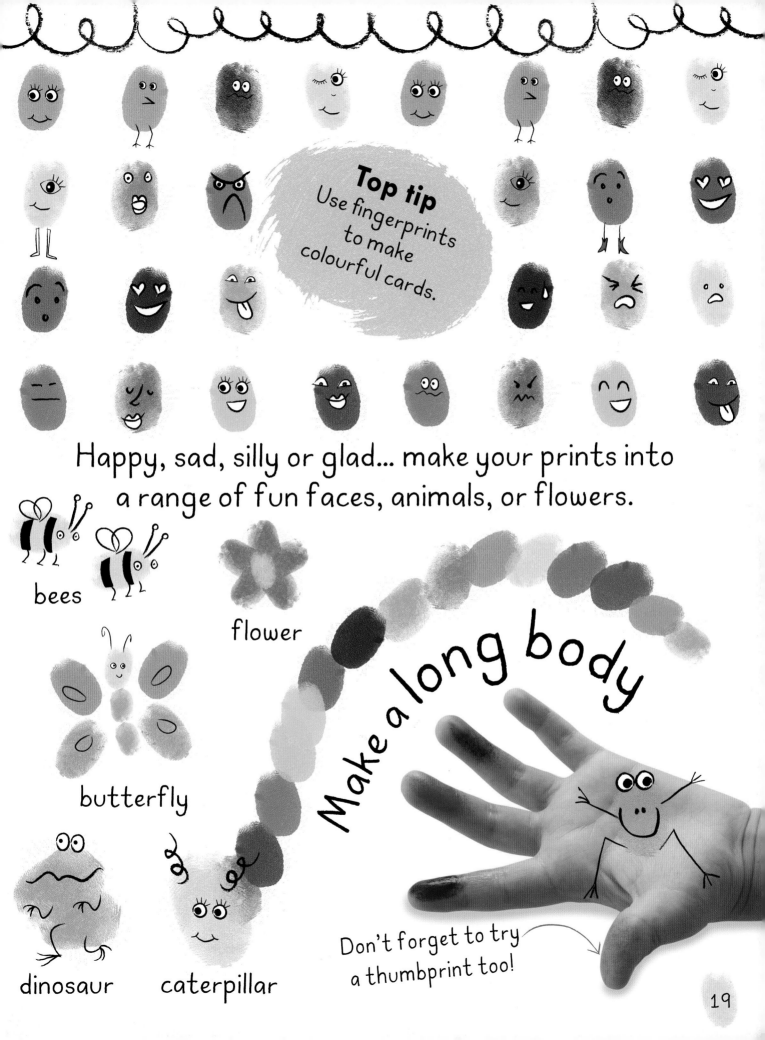

Top tip
Use fingerprints to make colourful cards.

Happy, sad, silly or glad... make your prints into a range of fun faces, animals, or flowers.

bees

flower

butterfly

Make a long body

dinosaur

caterpillar

Don't forget to try a thumbprint too!

19

Hedgehog

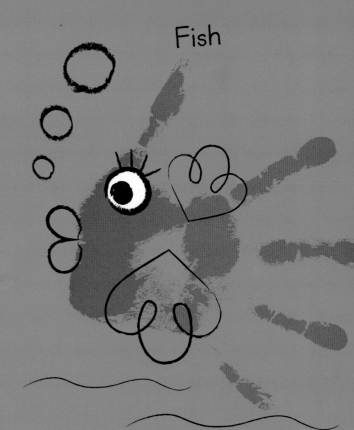

Fish

Use your **hands** to make **funny** animals!

Handy hands!

Paint your hands and press them onto paper.

Once the prints are dry, use a pencil to draw on eyes and other features.

Flamingo

Chicken and chick

Handy hint
Make your picture into a whole zoo of handprint animals!

I have hands for feet!

Elephant

21

Funny feet!

Make mess-free **clean feet** art using paint inside a bag.

Tools needed:

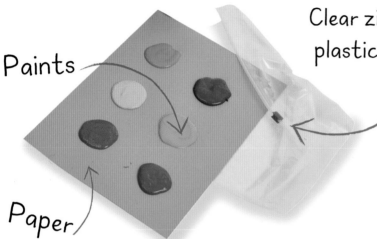

Paints

Paper

Clear zip-up plastic bag

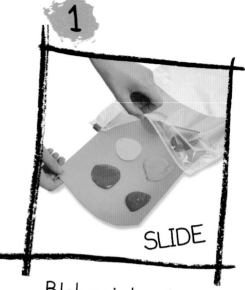

1

SLIDE

Blob paint onto your paper. Carefully slide the paper into the bag.

Dip your feet in **paint** and make **messy feet** footprint art! Use a pencil to turn the footprints into pictures.

Mess alert!

Bee

Flip-flops

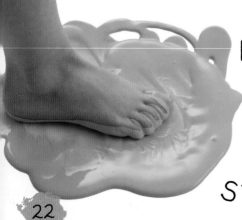

Feel the paint **squelch** between your toes!

STOMP!

Unicorn

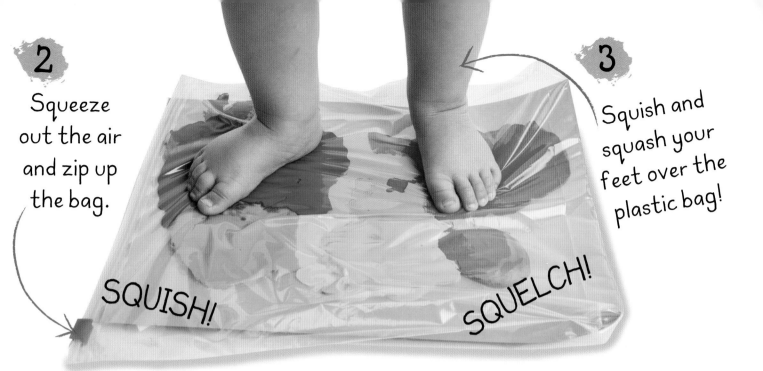

2 Squeeze out the air and zip up the bag.

3 Squish and squash your feet over the plastic bag!

SQUISH!

SQUELCH!

Now take out the piece of paper and look at your masterpiece.

hoot!

hoot!

Owl

grrr!

Cat

Lion

Bear

Butterfly

Lizard

Try a stripy print.

23

Pop! Art

Splatter your canvas and make some seriously splashy art!

Tools needed:

Balloons

Balloon pump

Funnel

Masking tape

Non-toxic paint

Mess alert!

This activity is MESSY, so it's best to do it outside!

Canvas (or thick paper)

1
FILL IT UP

Put the funnel into a balloon and pour in paint. Fill up about half the balloon.

2
PUMP IT UP

Take out the funnel and wipe away any paint from the balloon before pumping it up. Ask an adult to help you.

3

Fill more balloons with other colours.

STICK IT DOWN

Tie the balloon, then stick it onto your canvas or paper with tape.

4

POP!

With adult help, POP the taped-down balloons using a pencil.

Top tip
Try pouring two colours into one balloon.

SPLAT!

Remove the tape and deflated balloons.

SPLOSH!

Masking out

This is when you **stick down** tape or shapes and paint **over** and **around** them.

Tools needed:

Top tip
Try masking out with the shapes you cut out in the activity on page 36.

Canvas
(or thick paper)

Paints

Masking tape

Paintbrush

1 Stick down criss-crossing lines of masking tape on your canvas.

2 Paint your canvas. Don't worry if you paint on top of the tape.

3 When the paint is dry, peel away the tape to reveal a picture of lines and shapes.

27

Paper craft

Find out some of the **clever** things you can do with paper.
Here are the tools you'll need:

Paper: you can cut it, fold it, wet it, shine light through it...

Paper and card

Tissue and crepe paper

Water spray bottle

Pipe cleaners

Ruler

Wooden pegs

Masking tape

Googly eyes

Ribbons

Pencils

Glue

Felt-tip pen

Glue stick

You also need a torch!

Straws

Scissors

28

Paper folding

Transform paper into **3D** shapes with folds and curls.

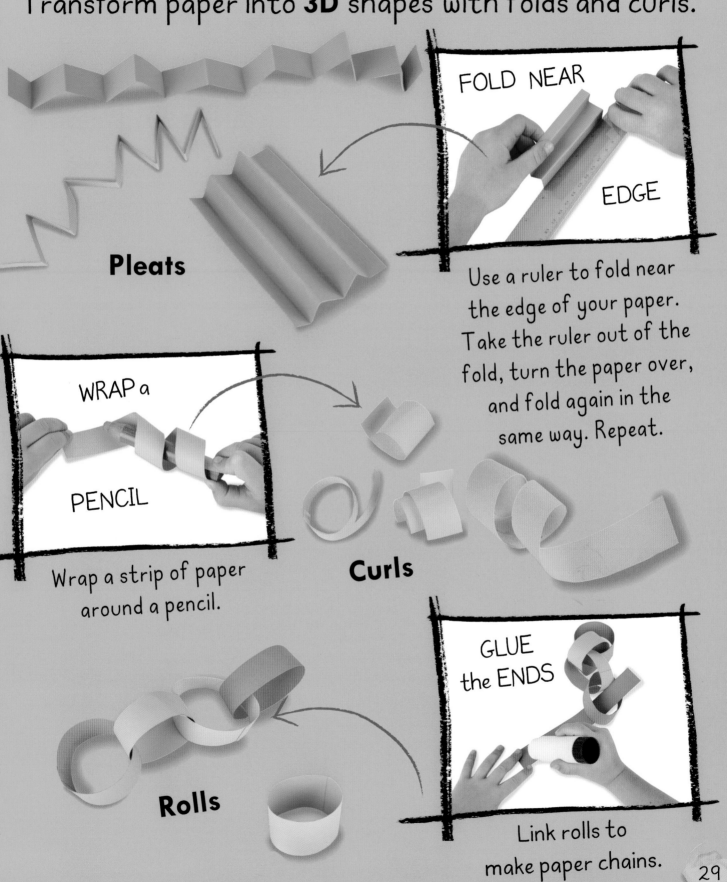

Pleats

FOLD NEAR

EDGE

Use a ruler to fold near the edge of your paper. Take the ruler out of the fold, turn the paper over, and fold again in the same way. Repeat.

WRAP a

PENCIL

Wrap a strip of paper around a pencil.

Curls

GLUE the ENDS

Rolls

Link rolls to make paper chains.

Paper cutting

You can make some great paper effects with just a few snips here and there!

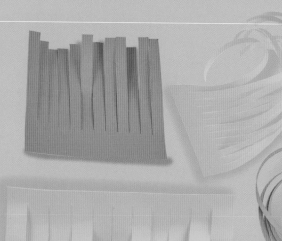

Fringes

SNIP to make a FRINGE

Make little snips along one edge of some paper. Don't cut all the way to the other side.

Draw a spiral to help you cut it out.

Spirals

CUT to make a SPIRAL

Cut into the edge of a circle and keep cutting round and round working towards the middle.

Draw eyes on the middle of your spiral to make it into a curly snake!

Paper sculpture

Use your folding and cutting techniques to create a colourful paper sculpture.

Gather your paper creations.

What other paper shapes can you make?

Glue your paper bits...

...onto thick card.

Paper caterpillars

Make these cute caterpillars with just a bit of **folding** and **sticking**!

Tools needed:

Strips of coloured paper

Pencil

Googly eyes

Glue

Scissors

Pipe cleaners

1

OVERLAP

Make a corner shape with two strips of paper. One piece needs to overlap the other.

2

Fold over

Now fold up

Fold the underneath piece over the other strip. Now fold the other piece up and over in the same way.

3

Keep folding until you run out of paper.

Top tip
Always fold the underneath piece.

Pipe cleaner antennae

You have a lovely smile!

Googly eyes

Now make a face for your little critters.
Glue eyes and antennae onto a square piece of paper, and draw on a smile.

Stick your face to one end of the body.

Fan-tastic!

Keep cool on a hot day with these funny face fans.

Tools needed:

Coloured paper

Coloured pencils

Pipe cleaners

Wooden pegs

Ribbons

Glue stick

Scissors

Ruler

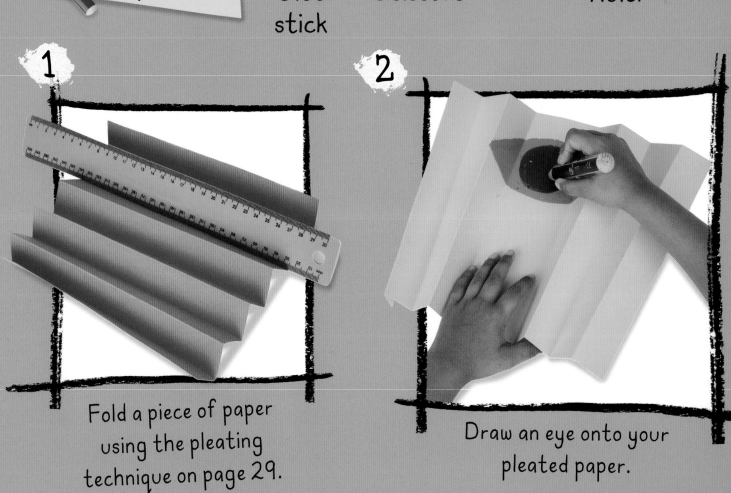

1

Fold a piece of paper using the pleating technique on page 29.

2

Draw an eye onto your pleated paper.

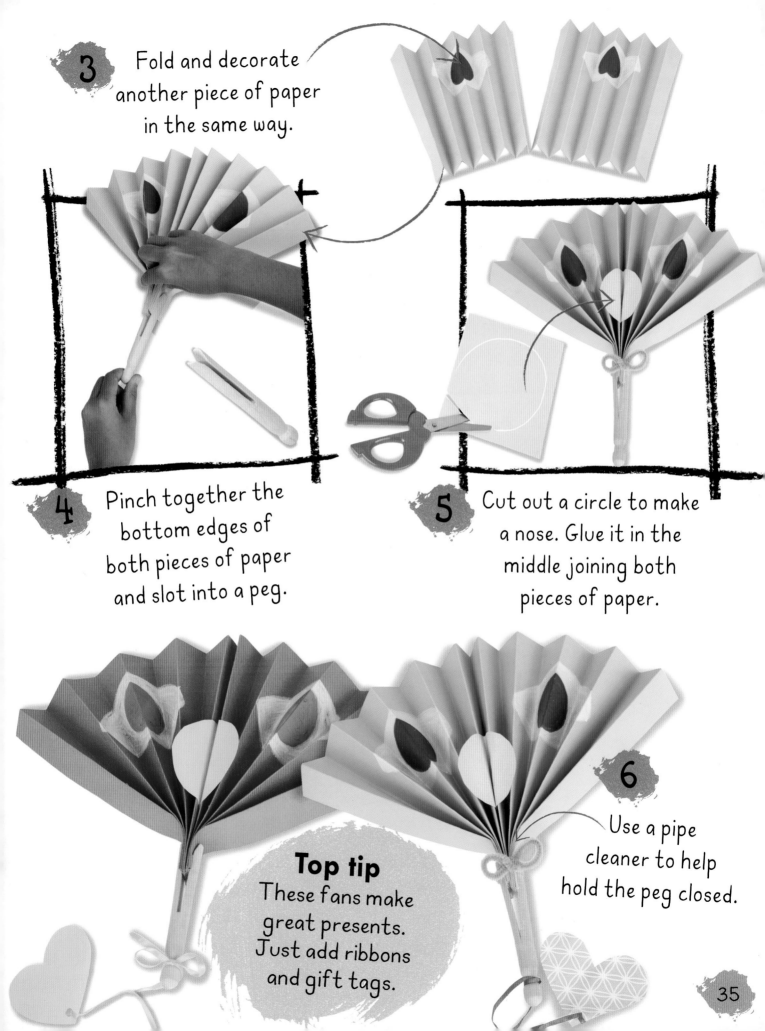

3 Fold and decorate another piece of paper in the same way.

4 Pinch together the bottom edges of both pieces of paper and slot into a peg.

5 Cut out a circle to make a nose. Glue it in the middle joining both pieces of paper.

6 Use a pipe cleaner to help hold the peg closed.

Top tip
These fans make great presents. Just add ribbons and gift tags.

35

Shadow puppets

Create a shadow scene with these easy-to-make **paper puppets.**

Tools needed:

Masking tape Scissors Black paper White pencil Straws

1

Top tip
Find templates at the front and back of the book to make your puppets.

Draw a puppet shape onto black paper and cut it out.

2

Attach a straw handle
with tape.

Hold us up near
a wall and
shine a torch at us.
Can you see our
shadows?

Stained glass
elephant

What other stained glass animals shall we make?

Hang this elephant in a window and see how the sunlight shines through the thin tissue paper.

Tools needed:

Black card

Tissue paper strips

Scissors

Glue stick

Felt-tip pen

White pencil

Use the stencil from the front cover of the book to make your elephant.

1

CUT OUT

Draw round the elephant shape. Ask an adult to help you cut it out.

2

STICK

DOWN

Stick your strips of tissue paper over the elephant-shaped hole.

3

Draw an eye and an ear on your elephant with a black felt-tip pen.

Top tip
Decorate your picture with screwed-up pieces of tissue paper.

Wet paper art

See how the colours **mix** and **run** when you spray water onto crepe paper.

Tools needed:

White paper
or card

Water spray
bottle

Crepe paper cut
into shapes

1

squirt!

squirt!

Spray water onto your
white paper.

2

ADD crepe shapes

Place your coloured
shapes on the wet paper.

40

3

Top tip
Use lots of layers of wet crepe paper to make your picture extra colourful.

Look at how the colours run into one another.

When you have filled the white paper with coloured shapes, spray more water on top.

4

When the crepe paper pieces are almost dry, peel them off.

Why not use your creation as wrapping paper?

41

Drawing and colouring

Practise your drawing skills and discover how to create different colouring effects.

What sort of picture shall we draw?

Tools needed:

Paintbrush

Lollipop stick

Black paint

Paper plate

Washing-up liquid

Chalks

Pencils

Felt-tip pens

Black and white paper

Crayons

Use **pencils**, **pens**, **crayons**, or **chalks**
to make lots of different **marks!**

Shading   Circles   Sparkle   Small circles   Dots

Zigzags   Spiral   Cross-hatching   Dashes

Wiggles   Squiggles

Use a squiggle to draw my hair!

Draw a **picture** with just one **line.**

Keep your pencil on the paper, and don't stop!

43

Animal doodles

Learn to draw animals with these simple steps. Build your picture shape by shape.

Practise the shapes on scrap paper first.

Sausage dog

1

Draw a long sausage shape.

2

Now add a potato-shaped head, a tail, and four legs.

3

Finish off by adding ears, claws, and a face.

All this talk of sausages is making me hungry!

Sleepy cat

1

Draw a curved
bean shape.

2

Now add a round head.

3

Next, draw four
legs and a tail.

4

To finish, add ears,
claws, and a face. Don't
forget the whiskers!

Singing bird

1

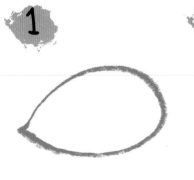

Draw a
balloon shape.

2

Next add leaf-shaped
feathers for a tail, and a
small balloon-shaped wing.

3

Finally, give your bird
legs, eyes, feet – and a
beak so it can sing!

45

Chalk art

Create your own **cheeky chalky aliens.**

What planet are they from?

Try rubbing chalk on its side.

Scratch art magic!

See colours appear as if by magic with scratch art drawings.

WOW! It must be magic!

Tools needed:

Paintbrush

Scratch with a lollipop stick or the end of a pencil

Black Paint

Lollipop stick or a pencil

Dollop of washing-up liquid

Plate

Paper

Crayons

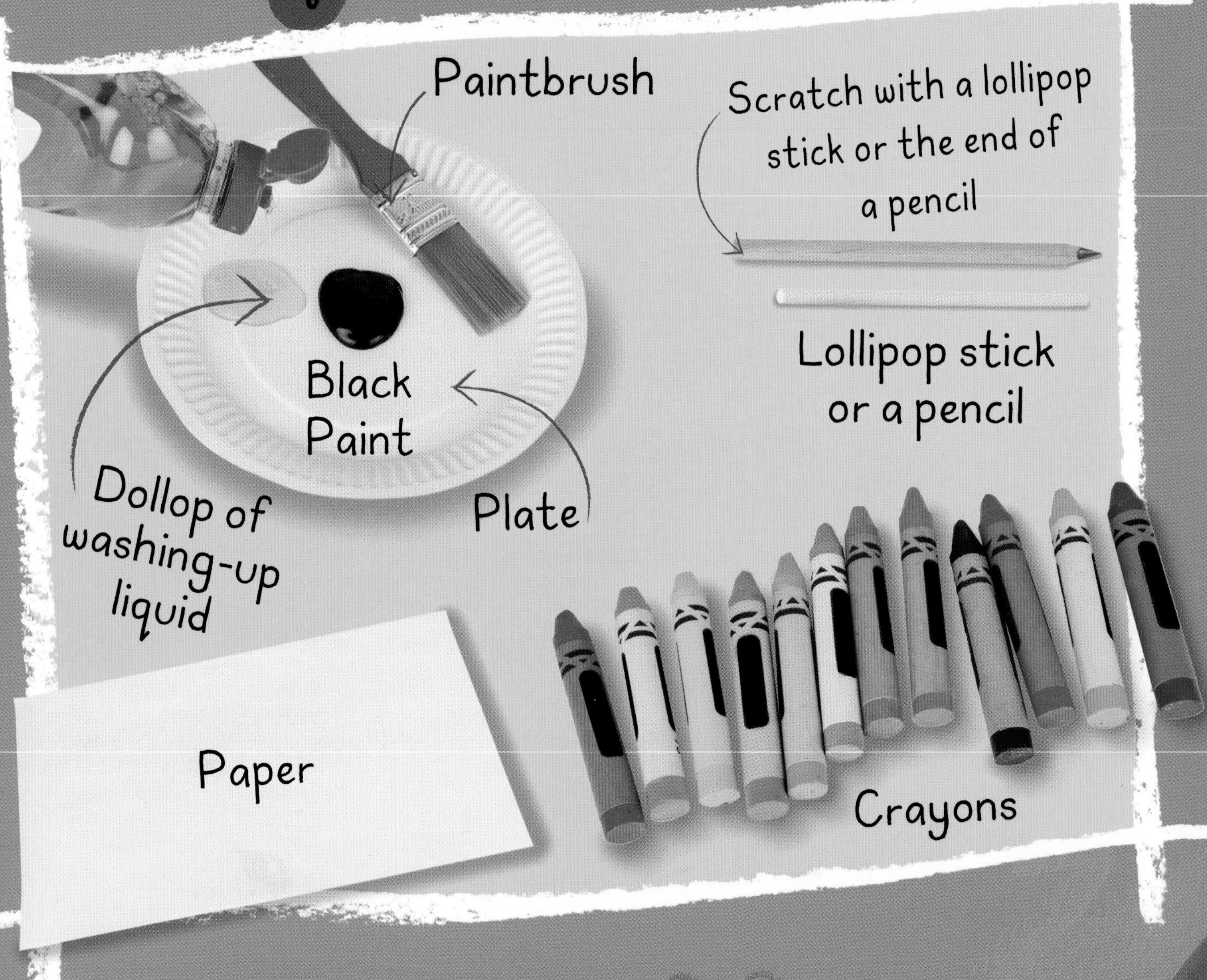

1

Colour a pattern onto
a piece of paper.
Use lots of colours.

2

Mix together the black paint
and washing-up liquid. Paint
over your crayon picture
and leave to dry.

3

Scratch a
drawing
into the
black paint.

Top tip
The more colours
you use, the more
magical your
picture will look!

Lollipop
stick

49

Make and create

Turn ordinary household items into amazing art.

Colour matching game

Practise your colours with this fun **game**. You'll need your colour wheel from page 11.

1

Cut out each section of your colour wheel.

2

Go on a hunt for coloured objects!

3

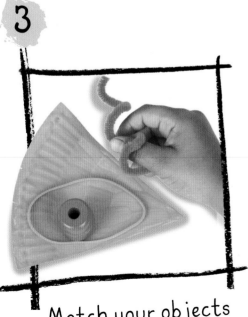

Match your objects to the colour of each section.

So colourful!

A tower of **tubes**

Paint cardboard tubes and slot them together to make a towering fort.

How high can you build your towers?

1

Cut cardboard tubes to different heights.

Paint your tubes in bright colours.

2

Add windows and patterns with white paint.

3

Cut two slits at the top and bottom, and slot your tubes together.

Rainbow mobile

Create a colourful cardboard mobile.

Tools needed:

Red   Orange   Yellow

Green   Blue   Indigo   Violet

Paints

Lollipop stick

String

Scissors

Wooden beads

Felt-tip pen

Corrugated cardboard

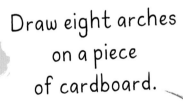
Paintbrush

1 Draw eight arches on a piece of cardboard.

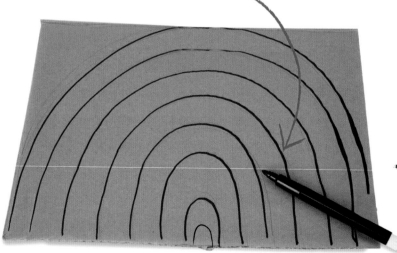

2

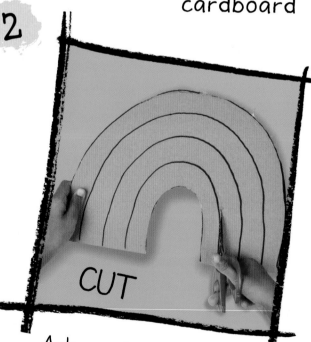
CUT

Ask an adult to help you cut along the lines. You should be left with seven arches.

3

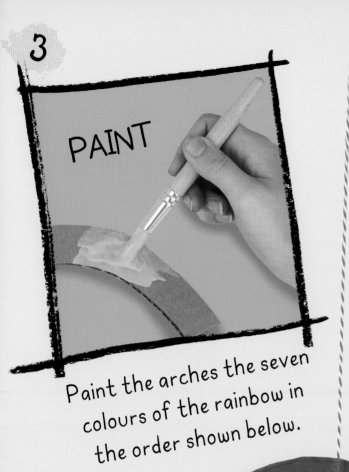

PAINT

Paint the arches the seven colours of the rainbow in the order shown below.

4

Lollipop stick

THREAD string

Ask an adult to help you poke a length of string through the top of each arch from biggest to smallest.

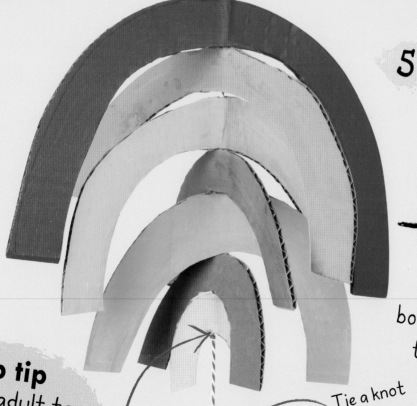

5

THREAD

Thread some beads on the bottom of the string to weigh it down.

Top tip
Ask an adult to help you hang your mobile in your bedroom.

Tie a knot here.

Tie a knot here.

Tie a knot here.

Watch it spin!

Magical unicorn

Find head, horn, and ear templates at the back of the book.

Make your own magical, fantastical unicorn hobbyhorse!

Tools needed:

Turn to page 30 to see how to fringe your card.

Fringed coloured card

Stapler

Horn cut from sparkly card

Glue stick

Scissors

Horse head shapes

Cut two head shapes out of white card.

Ears

Pencil

Paintbrush and paint

Long cardboard tube

1

PAINT your cardboard TUBE

Paint your tube in a nice bright colour. This will be your unicorn's handle.

2

Glue around the edges of both head shapes but not the bottom of the neck. Stick the fringed card, ears, and horn between the two.

Draw me a face and give me fringed card eyelashes.

3

Staple the two head shapes at each corner of the neck. Push the tube up through the gap in the middle.

Gallop around on your magical unicorn!

Top tip
Why not glue on glitter and sequins for extra magical sparkle?

57

Shadow theatre

Make a theatre and put on a **shadow show** with your **puppets** from page 36.

Tools needed:

Ruler

Cardboard box

Scissors

Masking tape

Felt-tip pen

Lamp

Glue

Tracing or baking paper

Hold us up at the back of the theatre.

1

Cut away one of the long sides of the box.

Draw a rectangle on your box. It should be about the width of a ruler away from the edges.

2

CUT

Ask an adult to help you cut out the rectangle.

3

Tape tracing paper to the inside of the box covering the hole.

Light your theatre from behind with a lamp.

4

Cut out and decorate pillars and a pediment. Glue them to the front of the theatre.

59

Cardboard collage

Make a city scene with scraps of **paper, fabric, and cardboard.**

Tools needed:

Googly eyes

Paintbrush for glue

Paints

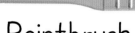

Paintbrush

Cardboard, coloured paper, and fabric scraps

Tinfoil

Masking tape

Glue

Scissors

Felt-tip pens

Shiny **fish**

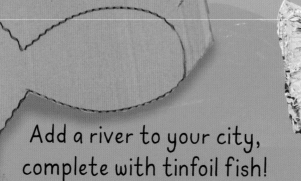

Add a river to your city, complete with tinfoil fish!

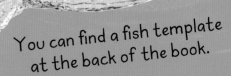

You can find a fish template at the back of the book.

City scene

Cut out your cardboard shapes and glue on your paper and fabric pieces.

Paint window panes and other details.

Use coloured masking tape to create windows.

Use different materials for doors.

Patterned paper can look fun too.

Use felt-tip pens to decorate us.

Glue on googly eyes.

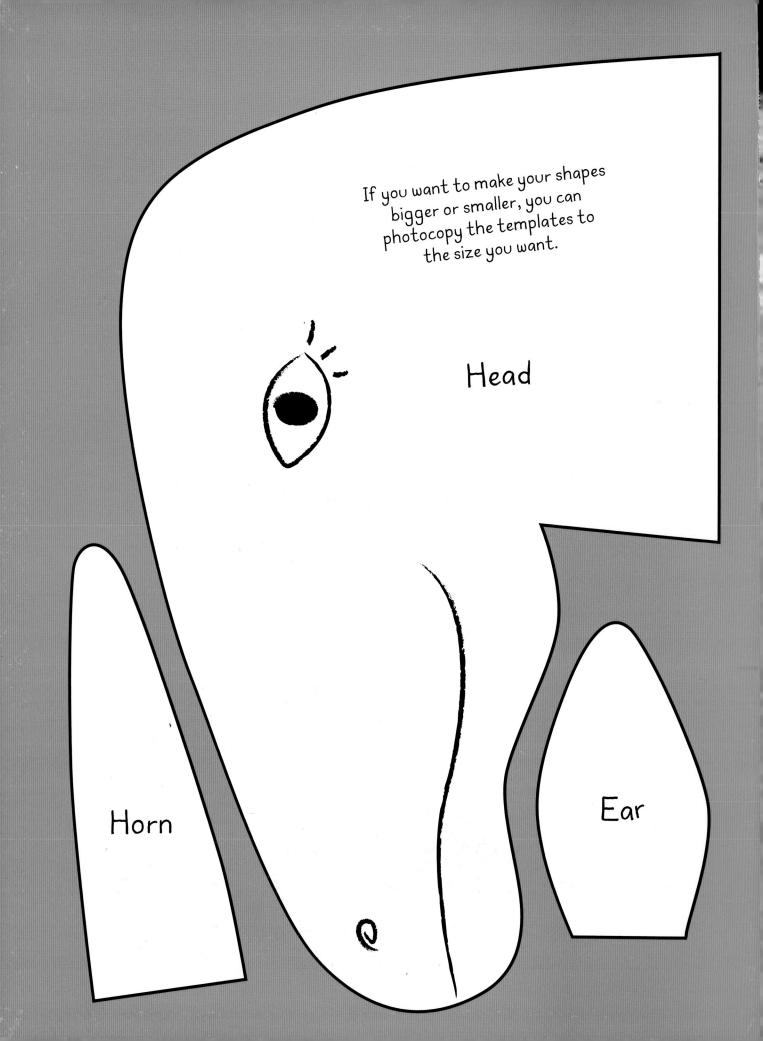

If you want to make your shapes bigger or smaller, you can photocopy the templates to the size you want.

Head

Horn

Ear